MW00800633

BETTER GOLF
BETTER LIFE

Better Golf
Better Life

LESSONS FROM
DR RICH GOLF

Richard J. Goldberg, MD

Unlocking the
transformative power of golf

The Library of Congress has cataloged this edition:
Goldberg, Richard
Better Golf Better Life:
Unlocking the Transformative Power of Golf/
Richard Goldberg, MD

pages cm.

1. Golf – Psychological aspects
2. Golf – Training

Library of Congress Number: 2022923220

ISBN: 979-8-9874529-0-5 (hardback)

This book is not intended to take the place of medical advice from a trained medical professional. Readers are advised to consult a physician or other qualified health professional regarding treatment of their medical problems.

DEDICATION

To those who taught me about
"Better Golf Better Life"
long before
"Better Golf Better Life"

Lao-tzu
Paul Brunton
Anthony Damiani

CONTENTS

Prologue

IN THIS BOOK, I am going to discuss a different approach to playing better golf. I'm also going to tell you how this new approach to golf can change your life. It may surprise you to hear that:

Your golf game will improve when you start to play golf to become a better person, not just a better golfer.

Golf is many things to many people. Whatever brings you to this great game, there is no wrong door. A round of golf brings your entire psychology and philosophy of life into play. You may have found yourself asking some of the following questions: "Why can't I get better at this game?" "What does my golf game say about who I am?" "Can I ever be satisfied with my game?" "Why do I sometimes feel like quitting?" "Why does my good golf abandon me just when I think I figured it out?" Even the greatest golfers are faced with these questions. Golf provides an ideal learning laboratory, with endless opportunities to uncover answers to your individual queries about the game along with a deeper understanding of yourself and the world.

Throughout this book, you will find perspectives that foster a greater sense of personal equilibrium and harmony made accessible through golf. You will also find that your golf game will improve. It is my hope and belief that after reading this book, you will understand why "You don't have to shoot a low score to be a great golfer."

Introduction to Dr Rich Golf

Dr Rich Golf was forged from a lifetime of golf, personal inquiry, and professional work. Throughout my 45-year career in psychiatry, I have learned how people can fundamentally change and grow. During 25 years of competing in marathon and triathlon, I gained a true understanding of how to mobilize performance psychology. For the past 50 years, I've thoughtfully engaged with meditation, mindfulness, and the study of Eastern philosophies, all of which provide invaluable skills that can help golfers of every level.

About fifteen years ago, the movie "Caddyshack" inspired me to establish the Dalai Lama Golf Association (DLGA) with a few of my golfing friends. At that time, there wasn't much of a philosophical foundation to the group other than an occasional reference to one of the film's greatest lines surrounding golf, "All you need to do is to get in touch with the force that makes things happen." After a few years, I began to feel that there was something far more substantial to this line than some good humor. Inspired, I undertook a serious consideration of the tremendous potential I saw in golf's ability to transform people's lives. Thus began Dr Rich Golf as my avocation over the last ten years. I have since grown the enterprise through my own learning and working with many exceptional clients.

This book emerged from the testimonies, stories, and what the students of Dr Rich Golf found of value as they began to transform themselves and their golf game. Golf forces us to balance technical, emotional, mental, and spiritual dimensions, all of which are addressed throughout this book's chapters. Each short essay is designed to be read in any order. You may find value in absorbing them one at a time and allowing each to methodically settle into your mind. Regardless, some of the essays will cater toward the practical, while others are more thought provoking and geared toward catalyzing change.

These essays have applications for every age and every level of golfer. I wanted to create a book that would be easily digestible to all, regardless of skill or current ability. I have worked with aspiring Monday PGA qualifiers, golfers trying to move up their state rankings, as well as mid to high handicappers wanting to better their game and feel more comfortable on the Green. A growing category of Dr Rich Golf clients consists of aging golfers who are trying to figure out why they are continuing to play this game when they can't hit the ball as long or score as low as they once did. In short, wherever you are in your golf journey is the accepted starting point, and you truly don't even have to play golf to understand the lessons in this book, though it will likely be more engaging if you are familiar with golf, or with someone who is.

Just like the game itself, one quick run through of this book will not master its contents. My hope is that you may connect with a few of the provided sentiments that can make you a better golfer and… a better person. Furthermore, while some readers may find themselves more engaged with certain essays than others, I would like to encourage you to start with the first five chapters and then explore any contents that you feel most drawn to. We're all on different parts of the path, after all.

1

The Fundamental Importance of Self-Awareness

I KNOW YOU WANT to shave some strokes off of your handicap. I know you want to hit your drives ten yards farther, or at least two yards farther than your golf buddies. Perhaps you even want to page through this book and scan it for a few golden golf tips for the mental side of the game.

However, simply consuming another quick golf tip is not going to help you, and I'm sure that you've already gone through hundreds of them! Maybe they do stick for a day or two, or even a little longer, but eventually, you're right back where you started, hungry for the next hot tip without any sustainable progress. This transient addiction leads to a cycle of frantically going through golf magazines, late night YouTube videos, or buying the latest game improvement device that you eventually grow past and discard into your collection of old clubs and putters in the garage.

So, what should you do instead? Hit the pause button on that search for quick tips, and ask yourself the key question:

What do I need to learn about myself to play better golf?

There is no reason to remain stuck in the same patterns as another golf season goes by or to continue to feel as if "I just can't score the way I think I should" despite investing in more lessons, equipment or the latest clickbait headline. There is a legitimate, and impactful way to move forward, and Bobby Jones famously told us how:

"Of all the skills needed in golf, self-inquiry is the most important."

Your real golf improvement journey begins with a fundamental practice—a willingness to take an honest look at yourself. A new world awaits those golfers who open themselves up to self-inquiry.

$=2=$

Breaking the Chain of Excuses

FOR GOLFERS WILLING to look inwardly at themselves, the best place to start is to begin the process of breaking the chain of excuses. Think about the most common reaction to missed shots for many golfers—making an excuse. When something goes wrong, we reach into our pocket and come up with some variation of the following: the sun is too bright, the shadow bothered me, I was distracted by the sprinkler head, I can never hit from a downslope, that person is in my head, I was up late last night, someone was talking, these new shoes are too tight, the caddy gave me the wrong club, I'm not strong enough or fast enough, I'm too old, I'm too young, I don't have enough time to practice, and so on.

When something goes wrong for great golfers,
they first turn around and look at themselves.

While making excuses can be an incredibly human thing to do, it hinders us from unleashing our full potential. It's far easier to blame the wind than it is to learn how to play in windy conditions. It takes courage to face the reality of your own behavior because if you can't blame something else, what's left? You're then required to mindfully take note of your own actions and to fully acknowledge who you are. Remember, the goal is not to judge yourself harshly but to relieve yourself of any facade or hindrance within the game for your ultimate improvement. Once you start to take note of your own use of excuses, I guarantee that they will become apparent rather quickly.

Try catching your excuse in real-time right after a poor shot outcome. When you spot it happening, rather than blaming yourself, you can start to disempower excuse making by smiling and employing some positive self-talk reflection, "I still have a long way to go. Next time will be different. What do I need to learn to have a better outcome next time?" As you make this shift in your personal dialogue, you will not only begin to break the cycle of excuses on the course but naturally bring this conscientious attitude into your everyday life. Your commitment to looking inwardly jump-starts the process of becoming a better golfer and a better person.

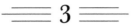

3

Stop Overreacting

GREAT GOLF EMERGES from an integrated and balanced orchestration of multiple brain functions. Emotional and physical overreactions to problems on the golf course disrupt that balance and make it impossible for us to perform at our best. The most blatant overreactions are obvious: slamming, breaking, or throwing a club. Less dramatic examples include expletives, grunts and groans following a missed shot or carrying negativity with you after a missed shot.

Short of the unacceptable club-throwing, what's really so bad about emotional displays of reactivity? We see displays of frustration every week on the PGA broadcasts, and the announcers sometimes debate whether slamming a club is really a problem or simply a healthy release that helps a player move on instead of holding things in. When you're playing at the level of the PGA tour, you can argue that slamming a club from time to time helps you rebalance. Elite performers are able to emotionally re-center themselves more quickly and successfully than most people. For the rest of us, let's acknowledge that overreactions are not so much therapeutic, but rather feed into an underlying instability and create clouds that follow us around for a while. Overall, maintaining emotional equanimity is a far better practice for good golf.

Acknowledging and owning our own over-reactivity is the first step towards achieving equanimity, which is a *sine qua non* of the elite golfer. The ubiquitous overreactions that occur in everyday life can easily become established as "normal" in a world filled with irritants. The goal is to actively move away from this mentality. The second step is to attempt to replace overreacting altogether by substituting it with self-regulation—taking a deep breath (or two). Remember the old adage about counting to 10? It works. The transformation from "hothead" to a calmer competence is possible if you're ready to take a moment and, yes, breathe. I've seen many clients make this intentional switch and each time their golf games improved.

I once worked with a surgeon who took me by surprise the first time I saw him throwing his club after topping a fairway bunker shot. Eventually, he acknowledged that his temper could be a problem that was limiting his game. He made the decision to dedicate himself to learning some basic breathing techniques that helped him recenter himself. Soon after, he began breaking 80. Once he learned how to breathe, he learned how to score.

Another of my students reported a similar experience:

During yesterday's qualifier I hit an approach shot 20 yards over a green into the woods. My initial reaction was to catastrophize the situation. I had imagined that I was headed for a really big number and that my chances to make the cut were ruined. Instead of overreacting, I took a breath, calmed myself down, found the ball, punched onto the green, and made a putt for a par. I truly believe that the outcome would have been different without recognizing the problem in real-time and using some new skills to maintain my equanimity (see Chapters 13 and 14).

The resolve to cultivate equanimity and reduce over-reactivity is one of the most important decisions that aspiring golfers can make, and it's one that tends to have a ripple effect. Many golfers find themselves asking, "How and when am I overreacting in my life off the golf course? Am I overreacting to certain people at work, in the neighborhood, at home, in lines at the grocery store, or in traffic gridlock? Did something my partner say really warrant that angry reaction?" While managing over-reactions in daily life can prove far more complicated than a situation of a missed golf shot, the golf course provides a learning platform for developing regulation skills that carry into everyday life. As we make progress towards managing and controlling our overreactions, we begin to slowly establish a capacity for something even greater, the capacity for balanced self-modulation.

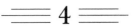

4

Slow Down

I LEARNED one of golf's most valuable lessons from a caddy at St. Andrews when I found myself in the infamous "Hell Bunker" on the 14th hole. The 112 bunkers at St. Andrew's, some of them so deep that you're lost in shadow, can break your game and your spirit. In his victory at the Open there in 2000 Tiger Woods did not go into a single one over his four rounds. Not so fortunate was Jack Nicklaus, who took four shots to get out of Hell Bunker in the opening round of the 1995 Open. One of the greatest names of all time, Bobby Jones, famously picked up and walked off the course after several attempts to escape the cavernous "Hill" bunker on the 11th hole in his third round in 1921.

Back in Hell Bunker, I was hitting my third shot from the sand before I knew it and I was setting up to whack my fourth. My mind and body felt shocked by this crushing turn of events, compounded by feelings of embarrassment. Heart racing, I started to move faster with each subsequent deteriorating swing. My caddy mercifully intervened, stating with sage-like compassion, "Laddie, when you start to lose your game, slow down." So, I stepped out of the bunker, knocked the sand off my shoes, and took a deep breath. I returned as if I were new to the situation entirely and was able to escape sideways onto the fairway. Slowing down and re-centering is as central to golf as it is to daily life, especially when things are not going well.

You may ask, "What good is slowing down if I have such a flawed bunker game in the first place?" Everyone has flaws in their swing. I'm not here to tell you that you can avoid learning proper basic golfing techniques just by learning how to slow down and breathe. Of course, you do need to know how to set up and correctly utilize the bounce on a sand wedge. However, without obtaining the skill set of slowing down, it's likely that knowledge will not be as effective as it could be.

More often than not, we are mindlessly speeding our way through life: getting chores done, rushing along shopping aisles, trying to find a parking spot, paying bills, trying to solve a computer glitch, reading dull work reports, getting through our call list, meal prep, or ticking off the "must-see" places on a vacation. Pretty soon some people find themselves rushing through a round of golf to get to the next thing on the list. We lose our equanimity and ability to engage with the present when we rush through a round simply to complete the next thing on our list. We can get away with this approach much of the time, but overall, rushing through life is not the best way to achieve happiness and it can even lead to hypertension and long-term stress-related health consequences.

═ 5 ═

It's Time to Own
Your Swing

YOU'VE PROBABLY HEARD the phrase "owning your swing." Maybe you assumed that this is only possible for very advanced players. After all, Tiger said that there were only two people in the history of golf who owned their swing: Ben Hogan and Moe Norman. Ben Hogan (1921–1997, 64 PGA tour wins and 9 majors) had so much control of his golf swing that he was legendary for his accuracy. Moe Norman (1929–2004), while less known, was said by Tiger Woods and Sam Snead to be the greatest and straightest ball-striker the sport has ever seen. Surprisingly, Moe was self-taught and never took a single lesson.

I'm here to tell you that owning your swing is not something that belongs to the elite few. It is something that every golfer can and should strive for. You already own your handwriting and individual way of walking and talking, etc., so why not your golf swing? While owning your golf swing requires some work—well, a lot of work—the rewards of doing so are no less than discovering a better golf game and understanding of yourself. So, what are you waiting for?

Now, what does it really mean to "own" your swing? Trevor Immelman (11 wins, 2008 Masters champion) commented on this during an interview with Claude Harmon, saying:

> If I could do it all again, one of the mistakes I made was that I didn't own my own swing. I was very reliant on other people telling me what to do, what to change, and why things worked and didn't work. I think it's so important to understand why your swing works. If you can do that, you have a better chance of fixing it when it gets a little out of whack.

Immelman's advice is to become more self-reliant when it comes to your golf swing. That doesn't mean you stop working with a teaching pro, but it does mean that you learn to be your own coach. He states:

If you don't know how to fix your golf swing your-self when things go wrong, you don't own your swing. All of us go through periods where we hit it great, then hit it terribly, then hit it great. We go through that wave all the time, and to me, the best ones can troubleshoot their own swing. They can fix stuff on the fly.

"Swing *your* swing" Arnold Palmer famously said. "Not some idea of a swing, not a swing you saw on TV, or a swing you wish you had. No, swing *your* swing." Owning your swing requires a commitment to self-discovery. "Self-discovery can be more powerful than someone telling you what to do," says Jason Guss, a Golf Digest Best Young Teacher. This philosophy is not only compelling but proven. The American Psychological Association examined more than 125 studies focused on success from autonomous learning versus external goal setting. The tasks varied, from shooting a basket-ball to computer skills and beyond, but the conclusion was certain: The rewards from self-directed exploration outweighed those from outside forces such as adopting what other people tell you to do. Figuring it out your-self also provides you the freedom to create a swing that feels natural.

So, what can you do specifically to start owning your swing? How you practice is the deciding factor. The most effective practice involves stepping away from reliance on authorities and learning to observe and then create the connection between your inner world and the outcomes you produce. You need to make your own decisions about what works best through repetitive experiments. In *The Golfer's Sixth Sense*, Markus Westerberg refers to golfers who practice this approach as "truth seekers." They look to their golf practice as a chance to learn about themselves and are not afraid of making mistakes or exploring potential dead ends. They are watchful for subtle clues of cause and effect and approach the game as a path toward inner discovery. As Westerberg says, "It is your responsibility to find out what helps you perform." This approach to practice becomes a lifelong journey that will create meaningful growth both on and off the golf course.

You begin by getting to understand your swing as it actually is today, not as you hope it will be in the future. Rid yourself of any simplistic or judgmental labels for your swing such as saying it's "good or bad." Common golf correction advice such as "keep your head down" "you're coming over the top" or "you need to finish your swing" are not going to be helpful if you don't take the time to figure out the deeper dynamics of the underlying problem. Equally, comparing yourself to others is not helpful, and it's best to consider your swing as being "in process."

In *The Talent Code*, Daniel Coyle talks a lot about what he calls "deep practice." He found that the most successful athletes and musicians practice with very focused attention and are willing to learn from repeated mistakes. Successful students did not immediately consider their practice to be automatic, natural, effortless, or routine. You will find that deep practice is exhausting and requires ruthless curiosity along with sharpened observation to see, hear and feel what is working and what is not. Deep practice requires tremendous concentration, and your sessions may sometimes differ in length depending on your ability to maintain focus. The payoff for deep practice is a swing that increasingly approaches a more automatic, natural, and effortless motion. This approach does not preclude engaging with a talented instructor—especially if you can find one who understands your interest in learning to own your swing.

Approach practice with patience and calmness. You should feel as though each session may or may not result in an immediate payoff. As with anything, the amount of time that you are willing to dedicate to honing your skill matters, whether that's 40 minutes, 4 hours, or 40 hours—but that should not stop you. Golfers are all at varying points in their journey. Only emerging high-level players and professionals are able to devote the time required to reach an elite level. Be curious, observant of outcomes, and willing to experiment. There is no rush.

Of course, many practice sessions will go by when you don't seem to achieve anything. That's normal. Ignore the little voice inside of your head telling you that it's impossible to teach yourself. Just go out and play using what you have and who you are. At some point, if your process is patient and sincere, you will learn something substantial. In turn, simply stating, "I found something on the range today" does not mean anything unless you have taken the time to absorb and own what you've found. Otherwise, it will evaporate, and the process begins again. There is an enormous amount of satisfaction in discovering something about your swing and process once you realize that it belongs to you—you own it.

Along the way, you will likely explore many aspects of your swing such as tempo, alignment, takeaway, swing planes, weight shifts, shot preparation, mental frameworks, and so on. How do you know if you're moving in the right direction with your practice? That's simple. Outcomes. Practice is meant to have practical effects. Your outcomes may be external, such as distance and accuracy, or perhaps physical, like balance, tempo, and swing length. They could also be internal, such as an improved capacity for visualization or positive thinking. Consider applying some data to narrow down an aspect of the game to explore in practice and perhaps utilize some game improvement devices thoughtfully. Devices can be helpful assuming you know what to do with the data. There are a lot of rabbit holes you can fall into with the torrent of data that they can produce.

The process of learning to own your swing involves adopting a thoughtful approach and an attitude towards practice and towards yourself. If you engage in deep practice, you will start to transform, not just in your swing, but in yourself. You may find this practice starts to carry over into a revitalized willingness to approach life with a greater sense of curiosity.

6

Battling Input Overload

Many golfers who are looking for ways to improve find themselves fighting input overload. We are barraged by advertisements promising that their new equipment will get us to hit it farther and straighter. While club fitting helps, where does it end? There are thousands of shaft options alone, each with a potentially different feel and possible result. One day I got a call from someone who said, "Dr Rich, in the last three seasons I've bought 6 sets of clubs, I have over 40 putters in my garage. Please help me before my wife throws me out." Then there are the endless reservoirs of YouTube instruction videos, Podcasts, articles, and an army of talented and capable professional instructors out there.

I also got another call one day asking, "Dr Rich, I used to be able to break 80 but now I can't even break 100. I have three teachers, and dozens of things going through my head every time I step up to the ball. Plus, all my friends are giving me their input. Can you help?" For many golfers, there is simply way too much going on. It's like they need to reset their hard drive because their brain is so cluttered, and who could blame them?

Jumping impatiently from one "fix" to another is counterproductive. It's easy to get overloaded with possible "fixes" and succumb to the idea that your "answer" is probably on the next page of the latest golf magazine or social media post. These endless inputs from the outside world that fight for our attention are difficult to ignore and ultimately leave us feeling more lost than we were before we engaged with them.

When people are floundering with input overload, I like to have them strip everything back to the roots. I begin by asking the player to play 18 holes without keeping score. Three rounds would be even better. Of course, throwing away the scoring pencil goes against every golfing instinct, but it's paramount for this exercise. On these non-scored rounds, I suggest simply keeping track of the number of good swings. Golfers generally know what their own good swing is unless they become too obsessional about it. It's important not to be too perfectionistic here.

Simply by focusing on creating good swings, with 3 swing thoughts maximum, most people start to play better golf with a clearer mind and a less cluttered swing process. It's important to allow yourself to enjoy the opportunity of going out and taking some good swings without the burden of scoring. Once you get an idea of how many good swings you generally produce in a round, you can set a goal of trying to produce a few more, without trying to balance so many priorities, expectations, and demands. If someone asks what you're up to, just say "I'm out here trying to take some good swings." That's all there is to it.

Since we play golf to be better people, not just better golfers, we can think about the input overload we experience in our everyday lives. The school of philosophy run by Pythagoras 2600 years ago required its students to look back at their behavior at the end of every day and to score their good and poor swings (he used other words of course). We, too, should reflect on each day to take note of our good "swings" and the problem "swings" we could improve on. Then take what you've learned and aspire to spend some time trying to take those good swings more often in your life.

7

Your Round Begins When You Wake Up

Y OUR ROUND BEGINS when you wake up and your opening tee shot is an extension of everything that led up to your arrival at that tee. Of course, sometimes you can jump out of the car, rush to the tee, hit the best drive ever, and stride down the fairway saying, "so much for practice." However, if you are serious about improving your performance on the first tee, you need to pay attention to how you begin your day.

How do we usually start our day? Many people wake up before the alarm with their minds already racing. Even for those who can sleep until the alarm goes off, the mental machinery gets into gear right on cue. Too many of us feel as if we are shoehorning some golf into an otherwise overpacked schedule. Even on days off, many golfers find themselves rushing. We rush to get dressed, wolf down some food, drive too fast to the course, blast through a locker room routine, smack some golf balls, and expect to be centered and balanced at a good tempo on the first tee. A minority of people are gifted with the ability to quickly transition into "performance mode." For most of us, we need to talk about the importance of slowing down.

So, what could we aspire for when arriving at the first tee? Ben Hogan talked about moving in slow motion before a round, to the extreme of slowing down his fork during breakfast. Phil Mickelson has talked about the value of morning meditation being especially necessary while trying to balance career demands with the focus required for winning. Most of us don't have to worry about juggling sponsors and our appearance schedules, but we all have demands that can feel just as hectic and overpacked. We continue to value how much we do instead of how well we do it. A renowned psychologist of the human spirit, Carl Jung, said that "One thing done with attention and feeling is more valuable than many things done in a rush."

Beginning our day in a better way is a good place to start. There are no mulligans in everyday life, and each morning is an opportunity. Most of us are guilty of launching ourselves into our day with a hyper-quick tempo, unbalanced breathing, and a body that is out of synch, stiff, and aching. Taking the time to invest in a better morning routine, in whatever way we can, will help correct those imbalances and will pay big dividends. Consider creating some new habit patterns for the morning. These could be as simple as five to ten minutes of mindful breathing or gentle flexibility exercises. If you're like most people, any routine change can feel like a gigantic hurdle to overcome, and it can be hard enough to simply get out of bed. However, any positive adjustment is possible and noteworthy. Consider starting your day with some brief (two-minute) meditation. You will be rewarded with clearer thinking and a boost in creativity, energy, and productivity. If it's a golf day, you will likely hit a better first tee shot and play better golf.

8

Before You Tee Off

WHAT DO YOU usually do before you tee off? Hit a few balls on the range and try to sink one 3-foot putt? Or perhaps nothing. Most of us don't have the time, don't make time, or don't bother with much of a pre-round routine. Many go to the range with their friends if everyone else is going. However, others trend the other way, maintaining elaborate and serious rituals on the range before a round. Have you ever considered what you could accomplish if you had fifteen minutes before teeing off? This is not a relevant question for a professional golfer or top competitive amateur who usually sets aside 60–90 minutes for a pre-game routine. For the rest of us *non-elite* golfers, here's one approach to a time efficient pre-game routine.

Warm-Up 5 minutes: If all you have is 5 minutes, the most valuable use of that time is to warm up your muscles, connective tissues, and joints. Accelerating the clubhead from zero to 70, 80,90,100 MPH or more after taking only a few swings on the first tee creates a risk for low-mid back tightness or even injury. When the low back tightens, you can no longer rotate freely, so the swing becomes all arms and then the misery begins. Golf is a sport, after all, and deserves the respect of a proper warm-up. For those of you getting a little older, this is even more important. So, let's embrace some physical warm-up before the round and ease into things. A few minutes with a warm up device like the "Orange Whip" can make all the difference. There are also numerous excellent sources on the Internet for warm-up routines for golfers. Take a look.

Practice Green 5 minutes: If you have another 5 minutes, spend it on the practice green for tempo tuning and getting some sense for distance control (see Chapter 16). Either assume that the practice green speed matches the speed out on the course or ask in the pro shop to be sure. Even five minutes on the practice green can be a good investment. Of course, we've all had great putting days when we skipped the practice green, and we've had terrible putting days even after making a series of short putts to "build our confidence." Don't focus on making putts. The lure of making a few putts to "build confidence" is a trap. If you try to make a few quick 3-footers and miss them, then what? Or, if you make them, what have you accomplished since you will be approaching actual putts with an entirely different routine on the course? This is also not the time for putting drills. Those sessions are for another time.

Driving Range 10 minutes: Approaches to the driving range before a round vary greatly. Some people just take a few swings with a few clubs, and they're done. Some people try to hit every club, and many want to be sure they end up hitting the driver last. Let's think through what purpose can be served by a few minutes on the range, beyond going just to admire the geometric beauty of that small pyramid of sparkling white practice balls. A lot of people I've interviewed say "I have to straighten some things out before I tee off today." Really? I thought. Ten minutes before a round, it is unlikely you are going to figure something out that you can incorporate into your swing. After all, this is not a real practice session (see Chapter 5). If you do manage to hit some great shots on the range, what do we often hear next? "I always hit it great on the range but can't take it to the course." There are many reasons for this, but one is very straightforward. Nothing carries over because what happens in a few moments on the range before teeing off has created nothing to transfer. No real learning has taken place. Brain "rewiring" requires deep practice.

Concerns about carry-over to the course should be considered irrelevant for the 5–10-minute warm up session. If these warmup swings result in some great shots, you may not carry those over, and if they aren't so great, it doesn't matter either. You're there to establish some flexibility and some feeling for tempo, above all. If you attend to those two things, you will have accomplished a lot. Using the pre-round driving range as a preview for the day just sets you up for problems whether you hit "good" shots or "bad" shots. So forget about where the ball goes, and absolutely ignore bad shots.

Start with whatever club you feel helps you to establish your best tempo. Notice how that tempo feels and try to link it with your breathing—slowly inhaling on the backswing, and smoothly exhaling to the end of a completed swing—never forcibly expelling your breath (see Chapter 11). Notice how good these swings feel and how you are more likely to remain in balance at the finish. Five minutes of this may be enough. By the way, swinging to establish tempo can be done almost just as well without going to the range.

Overall, these 15 minutes of warm-up, practice green, and driving range, approached in the right way, are great preparation for the round ahead. For those days that you do not have any time at all, don't fall into the trap of believing that unless you complete certain pre-game rituals you cannot play well. An experienced brain seems to be able to "flip" itself into the right state at any time because of long hours of prior conditioning. Whatever warm-up routine you engage in or ignore, the under-lying dynamics that determine why a particular round ahead is going to be one of the best or worst remain truly mysterious.

9

Thoughts on
Pre-Shot Routine

I N 2005, I followed Annika Sörenstam for an entire round at Mission Hills. She was, at the time, number one in the world and won the tournament that year for the third time by eight shots. We rarely get to follow one professional for an entire round, usually seeing them on TV only as the cameras cut back and forth across groups. What we fail to observe on TV is what I saw with Annika that day. She followed the same exact pre-shot routine (PSR) for every shot for the entire round. Do we incorporate that same consistency and commitment in our own golf? Likely not. Of course, we're not professional golfers performing as number one in the world, but if we want to play better golf, we must emulate this approach with our own version of a PSR. We need to grapple with our lack of discipline and other forms of resistance such as thinking that we don't want to hold people up, or we don't want to be seen as too much of a stickler. But most of all, we have to acknowledge that we either don't believe in its value or are unwilling to make the effort.

So, if you don't have a PSR, you need to develop one and use it for every shot. You should also start to use your PSR during practice range sessions in order to simulate actual playing situations. Pia Nilsson and Lynn Marriot, co-founders of Vision 54, a breakthrough program of golf instruction, famously described the pre-shot routine in terms of two phases: the thinking phase and the action phase.

The "Thinking Phase" takes place from behind the ball. It's where everyone thinks about things such as target, wind, lie, and strategy. More individualized components include core swing thoughts, and the use of visualization, feel, or sound. How does the shot look, how does it feel, how does it sound? By the end of this first phase, you should feel certain about your intention, your distance, your target, and your club selection.

One of the core benefits of the PSR is managing anxiety. Mental engagement with your PSR checklist occupies the mind and crowds out other thoughts that may lead to anxiety. There's no room for performance anxiety or anxious anticipation of some potentially bad outcome. A calming breath is a common tension and anxiety reducing component often built into the PSR. A calming breath is basically a full inhalation held briefly and then fully exhaled while simultaneously relaxing muscles and letting go of tension (see Chapter 10). Athletes and performers from all areas know about this.

The PSR engages us in a positive narrative instead of disruptive thoughts which interfere with the mind-body's inherent capability to orchestrate the extraordinary complexity of the golf swing. The PSR helps to avoid dwelling on doubt, a well-known swing killer. Some golfers talk about doubts as a "lack of commitment." What exactly is "commitment" and how do we exercise it? It's not accomplished by simply saying to yourself "now I am 100% committed, let's go." While that intentionality is aspirational, it is often eroded by our own inner distractions even before the swing has started. Being 100% committed may be defined as being fully engaged in the details of the PSR process, so much so that it will feel and look like a ritual of some sort.

The second phase of the PSR is the "Action Phase" where thinking, analyzing, and planning are completely absent. In this phase, the golfer holds a clear intention, remains committed to the PSR process, and executes the shot. Immersion in the process is the key. Some golfers say, "I do best when I don't think, don't grind, don't make such a big thing about it all—I just get up and hit it and that seems to work best for me." If this works for you—keep doing it. However, one day you may feel prompted to try another way. Nothing is set in stone.

Does the PSR sound like a lot to do? It can certainly seem that way when it is unpacked like this for analysis and learning. However, the goal is to create a PSR that actually only takes 10–15 seconds. In the beginning, you may only choose, alter, and utilize a few elements until you build a routine that is more automatic and efficient. While the PSR does not guarantee a positive outcome, the lack of one guarantees a lower probability of success.

Learning to be fully "present" with your PSR is another way of engaging in "learning to be mindful" (see Chapter 14). Mindfully going through the steps of your pre-shot routine is a skill that you improve with practice. It is the royal road to reach the "zone" of enhanced performance (see Chapter 29). When you're mindful in your pre-shot routine, any interference of other thoughts becomes quiet, so your brain's physical and emotional functions can integrate optimally. There's also a post-shot routine, but that's for another day.

$\equiv$ 10 $\equiv$

First Tee Jitters

How many of us have ever experienced the first tee jitters? I would venture to answer, "almost everyone at every level." One of my clients noted some common performance fears that plague many golfers on the first tee, such as, "I hope I hit it well, I don't want you to think I'm a lousy golfer. There may be some people watching and I don't want them to see me hit a terrible shot." Fortunately, there's a fairly straightforward approach to managing the first tee jitters and it doesn't take years of psychotherapy!

First tee jitters can often be eliminated (yes, eliminated!). Important components for preventing any initial issues actually begin before you leave home for your round (see Chapter 7) and before you step up on the tee in your pre-round warm-up (see Chapter 8). Still, no matter how thoughtful you have been preparing to get to the first tee, everything can seem to speed up once your group is called. Then there may be debate about who is teeing off and in what order, a lot of last-minute bantering over the teams or the betting—before you know it, your focus has dissipated. Let's keep it simple. Here is an abbreviated first tee routine that will serve as a guide in helping you remove the jitters altogether.

First, focus mainly on creating your desired tempo in those beginning practice swings. An overly quick tempo is one of the most common problems off the first tee and results from a combination of factors, one being that we're pumped up and think that we have to swing hard and fast to launch that long first drive. It can be hard for many golfers to create that small but all-important transition pause we need at the top of the swing, especially when we've been rushing before even getting to the tee (see Chapter 7). Studies generally show that optimal swing tempos have a 3:1 ratio comparing backswing to through swing times. It's worth experimenting to determine your optimal ratio because knowing your ratio will enable you to get yourself back on track when necessary. Sometimes programming a desired tempo can be accelerated by using feedback from a peripheral device such as deWiz.

Second, use breathing to manage your arousal level. Some golfers get so nervous on the opening tee shot that they shake. Breath control is the most effective approach to reducing the sympathetic nervous system hyper-arousal (e.g., rapid heart rate and/or tremor) associated with performance anxiety. For reference, watch the breathing routines of a basketball player at the free throw line. Take one or two cleansing breaths, followed by a calming breath, then head into your pre-shot routine (PSR). I define a **cleansing breath** as follows: Inhale a complete breath. Retain the air for a few seconds, pucker your lips as if you're going to whistle then exhale a little air at a time with considerable vigor. It should take about four to five short rapid sequential bursts of air to completely empty your lungs. I define a **calming breath** as follows: Slowly fill your lungs breathing in through your nose completely and be sure to drop your diaphragm to initiate the breath and then fill your lungs fully from bottom to top (if you do not understand how to initiate a breath by dropping your diaphragm, it's worth looking for a YouTube video that explains it graphically). Briefly retain the breath, then let the breath out through your mouth with a single full exhalation, expelling all tension. You may note that as your shoulders drop, you feel an overall sense of calm and readiness to engage in your PSR with far less tension. Then sync up your calmed breathing with your golf swing (see Chapter 11).

Third, start to engage with your PSR (see Chapter 9). Bring your PSR with you as you step onto the first tee, this is the place to use it. Establishing a sense of tempo and managing your breathing are the foundations. At this point you should feel confident from your dedicated practice and have your PSR down to no more than 10–15 seconds. Be true to your routine and immerse yourself completely. You may even find that you become calmly oblivious to everything going on around you on the first tee. The pre-shot routine is not only good for reminding the brain what it is about to do but also engages the mind so it cannot find any space for anxious thoughts, outcome goals, or fears to intrude. Put aside all that internal narration on needing to "bomb one out there." You don't need to extract a compliment on your opening tee shot to feel good about yourself and capable of playing a great round. Ignore what you hear from the TV announcers about how the first shot sets the tone for the round ahead. It's only one shot and many great rounds have followed weak opening tee shots, just as many not-so-great rounds followed a perfect opening tee shot.

Breathing Your Golf Swing

W HEN WE PLAY GOLF, breathing correctly is of paramount importance. Put aside some time to become more aware of your breathing. Start by observing whether your breathing is synchronized with your golf swing. It should be. On your backswing, smoothly and fully breathe in, reaching maximum inhalation at the top of the backswing. On your downswing, smoothly and fully exhale to the completion of the swing. See if you can allow a natural and easy breathing rhythm to flow in tune with the swing. The breathing cycle should be full but unforced. Indications of problems with your breathing include breath holding, forced inspirations or exhalations, or anything at all explosive. Complete the swing coincident with the full completion of the breath. Some golfers, usually the better players, seem to do this naturally and have done so for a long time. The rest of us need to train ourselves. Matching your breathing to your swing creates the most efficient alignment of muscle energy and through that synchrony, you will find yourself more likely to stay in balance. You may also notice that somehow you become filled with peaceful energy from each swing.

For the purpose of this exercise, do your best to be thoughtfully aware of your breathing and how it matches your swing, for every swing, including your putts. Eventually, this awareness will become natural as you establish a routine breathing pattern that matches each swing. There will be no intrusive thinking about breathing and your awareness of it will recede into the background unless you decide to return to it in the future to help you recenter yourself. Some golfers find that staying in touch with breathing is one of the best ways to stay alert, avoid distractions, and remain performance ready between shots.

At the first sign of any problems with your swing, one of the first things to do is to get back in touch with your breathing. Always start by taking a calming breath (see Chapter 10) and then get your breathing re-synchronized with your swing. Through identification with breathing, we can remain in the moment. When we remain mindfully in the moment (see Chapter 14), we are able to re-center ourselves and remove feelings of confusion or distraction.

$$=\!\!=12=\!\!=$$

The Brain Does Not Hear "No"

A lesson from neuroscience on picking a target

IMAGINE THAT you're standing on a tee and looking out over a dogleg right gracefully curving around one boundary of a lake, filling your vision on the right. You stand behind the ball taking the measure of the shot ahead and tell yourself "Don't go right." You may be especially concerned because you've been hitting high right fades on prior drives most of the day. Your well-meaning golf partner or caddy tells you as you approach the shot, with all good intentions of course, "Don't go right."

Here is an important principle of neuropsychology:
The Brain Does Not Hear "No"

What your brain just heard is "Go right." So, it's no big surprise when you hit a high right drive, and the ball sails out and splashes in the water. Have you noticed how often you end up in a big bunker, lake, woods, or out of bounds… exactly everywhere you have told yourself NOT to go? Well, it turns out that you're inadvertently contributing to that outcome by warning yourself where not to go because the brain does not hear "No."

Here's the corrective solution. If someone says, "Don't go right," process that as potentially useful information, but always follow it up with the positive command that your brain needs. An example of a good follow-up assertion after being told what not to do would be to say silently or even out loud "OK, now, I see a specific tree in the distance (or edge of a shadow on the fairway, or anything that is very specific) and that is my target." In fact, alert yourself every time you hear a "don't" warning about what not to do on the golf course. "Don't go out of bounds here." "Don't hit short." "Don't get near that pot bunker." The verbal traps are endless. Every time you catch yourself, accept that the warning has some value for your strategy, but then follow it up with a positive statement: "The middle of the green is good." "I'm going to that tall tree on the horizon." "My seven iron is the perfect club to land on this green."

You will see how good it feels to fill yourself with positive thoughts instead of weighing yourself down with a negative warning. The positive aura you create will often allow you to express your capabilities rather than constrain your performance.

13

Learn to Meditate:
Will This Be the Year?

*Meditation is simply training our state of being so that
our mind and body can be synchronized.*
Chogyam Trongpa Rinpoche

G OLFERS NEED to find a way to clear their minds and
become centered and focused, especially at that
critical transition of starting the pre-shot routine. Have
you thought about solidifying your ability to maintain
concentration by learning how to meditate? It is increasingly
common to hear that many high-level players are
discovering the value of meditation. Phil Mickelson credited
his meditation practice with helping him maintain
his focus and win the 2021 PGA.

There is no shortage of advice on how to meditate.
Simply Google "How to meditate" and you will find
enough listings to occupy you for years. Recently, while

waiting in line at a Whole Foods check-out, I counted no fewer than nine different magazines promising to help with meditation or mindfulness. Some magazines are wholly devoted to the topic, along with ads and testimonials for meditation paraphernalia. You will be advised to have the right cushion, clothing, music, incense, lighting, posture, breath technique, and the correct place to sit, way to sit, and direction to sit in—well, you get the idea. It sounds almost as complicated as the golf swing. In fact, our pursuit of meditation skills and a better golf swing can both become derailed by innumerable distractions. Instead of engaging in a practice that allows us to "rise above ourselves" we find ourselves right back in the world of our own preoccupations.

The highly regarded golf teacher Harvey Penick said, "Playing golf you learn a form of meditation. For the four hours you are on the course, you learn to focus on the game and clear your mind of worrisome thoughts. Golf has probably kept more people sane than psychiatrists have."

Let's try to strip away the mystical cobwebs and unnecessary specialized or proprietary terms that make it harder than necessary to approach meditation. Meditation is a word that encompasses many different practices. What you engage with will be your own decision—depending on your background, prior experience, and what you want to accomplish. While meditation can take the form of a relaxation exercise, it is not just about relaxation.

Many forms of meditation presuppose the ability to physically relax. Finding your own set of relaxation exercises is well worth the time not only as preparation for meditation but also for health promotion and stress reduction.

Below, you will read about many of the common ways that the term "meditation" can be used. As you begin to engage in practice, it's important to be aware of your specific intention with the various meditation techniques that you implement.

Your meditation can take the form of an exercise that develops improved mental control. Enhancing the ability to focus is well worth an investment of time which will pay dividends in golf and many other areas of life. Be prepared that the battle for mental control can be a long, drawn-out practice since the mind is by its very nature always on the move and decides on its own where it wants to go.

Meditation can also aid us in achieving the very opposite of striving for mental control, where it asks the practitioner to just watch everything go by without getting involved. That's often easier said than done because the mind has a way of creating images for us that are so fascinating that before we know it, we become lost in our daydreams. This form of meditation appears to require no effort at all, as paradoxical as that sounds.

Your practice may alternatively take the form of immersion in contemplation, defined as deep mental and emotional exploration of a single topic or object. Creative people in all fields achieve states of contemplation naturally, though facilitated access to this creative state can be cultivated by practice.

Meditation can be as simple as mindful breathing exercises. This approach serves as a wonderful entry point. Enhancing mindfulness through a focus on breathing is one of the best ways for golfers to begin the practice of meditation. Those who begin here will discover some early rewards in terms of enhanced ability to maintain concentration and lower excess arousal on the course. Chapter 14 addresses this form of meditation in more detail.

Meditation is not just about trying to feel good while you practice it, although that is certainly common. In fact, when you try to engage, you are more likely to encounter feelings of being bored, restless, or physically uncomfortable. You are in the process of taming your ego and mind, both of which are used to being in control and don't want anything to interfere.

Whatever approach to meditation you choose, you will likely benefit. Meditation can help you better manage and persevere through all kinds of situations, on and off the course.

Meditation fosters equanimity, one of the most important foundations of good golf. As you become more involved, you may notice that you even begin to smile more when facing the constant challenges that emerge on the course and in life. Meditation helps you gain perspective. Over time, it will change your world-view, and you will become more settled and more flexible.

In your golf game, meditation will help you get out of your own way and allow your best natural swing to emerge. It will increase your ability to both clear your mind and decrease the number of times you lose your concentration. In golf (as in life) so many things don't work out as we want them to. Meditation helps us to stay present and reconnect with our best capabilities under adverse circumstances.

Golfers all know about the stress of trying to finish a round of golf that's going well. Many great rounds seem to fall apart around the 16th or 17th hole when the mind is prematurely anticipating the finish line. In those times, everything is perceivably falling apart, and you just can't find a good swing anymore. Worse yet, it can feel impossible to even get away from that feeling. However, with some meditation practice under your belt, you will find it easier to stay in the moment and break away from negative feelings by maintaining your inner balance and calmness. Whatever else you're doing to play better golf, you cannot afford to forego learning about and practicing meditation.

14

Basics of Mindfulness Meditation for Golfers

Playing your best golf, according to Patrick Cantlay (interview published in Golf Digest, August 2021) is a result of having done the work with your swing and your short game—and probably most importantly, with your mind.

So, what is this "work with the mind" all about? While Patrick does not say exactly what his "mind work" consisted of, he did define the result: Staying completely in the present and focusing only on what's required at each moment. The practice of being present in the moment is often referred to as the practice of mindfulness.

So, let's talk more about what mindfulness is in a way that may be helpful to you as a golfer and person. This essay is intended as an introduction to some basic concepts that can serve as a foundation for further learning and practice.

Just for a moment, look at the never-ending series of thoughts that make up your experience. It's been estimated that every day you have about 70,000 thoughts. Most of them flow right by without any real effect or notice. However, some of these thoughts elicit reactions and some of these reactions create problems for us. A guiding principle of mindfulness is that it's not our thoughts that create our problems, but how we react to them.

The basis of mindfulness practice, which we can also call mindfulness meditation, is to simply watch your thoughts come and go without emotional attachment. This awareness of your thoughts without reacting to them is the necessary foundation for mindfulness practice. Some people mistakenly think that they are trying to stop their thinking. This is a misunderstanding. Just watch. "Quieting" the mind will happen on its own as a result of maintaining awareness in the present moment— awareness without judgment or resistance.

Paying attention to some aspects of breathing is the most common "anchor" for mindfulness practice, for several reasons. Our breath is always right here with us and is always taking place in the present moment. Also, our breathing pattern can have a direct calming or agitating effect on our experience and the function of our brain and nervous system. Calm breathing quiets our mind and body. Mindful, calm breathing practice creates beneficial brain changes that can be demonstrated on an MRI: reducing arousal activity in the amygdala and enhancing pathways associated with attention and concentration.

The benefits from mindfulness meditation practice will not emerge from only a few days of practice, but you will start to notice something even within a few weeks. So, try it out. Sit quietly and comfortably and pay attention to your breathing. Watch it come and go. There is no reason to try to wrestle with or regulate it. It will calm down by itself when it's observed. There is no need to get caught up in straining to adopt some specific cross-legged or uncomfortable posture. There is value however in sitting in a way that avoids slouching and keeps the spine straight. One helpful strategy to help focus is to narrow your attention to the sensation of the air passing through the nostrils. Alternatively, some people focus on the rise and fall of the belly. There are endless options. Pick any one of them and don't obsess that there might be a better one.

When you try to sit quietly and pay attention only to your breathing, expect some distractions. That's how it is for everybody. As soon as you notice that you are no longer only paying attention to your breathing and that you've become lost in other thoughts, guide your attention back to your breathing. There's no need to be self-critical about success or failure. Just patiently come back to paying attention to your breathing.

It can be helpful for the beginner to create an individual approach that feels possible to manage. Set a timer for 5 minutes and try to pay attention for that amount of time. After a few weeks, you may decide to extend it to 10 minutes—it may be harder than you think. Most people should feel OK about starting with 2 minutes. Remember, our thinking process is accustomed to having free-range activity and does not like to give up its autonomy without a fight. It would be most beneficial to engage in breathing practice every day, ideally at the same time. Do what you can: 3 blocks of 5 minutes/week? You will have to decide what works best for you per your own level of commitment, understanding that this is a skill that can only be mastered with practice.

The mindful breathing practice that you do at home establishes a foundation for mindful presence on the golf course, improving your ability to sustain focused immersion in the all-important "process" that is key to golf. The success of all great golfers depends on how they can sustain engagement with their process. The outcome of process engagement is that better scores "happen."

The benefits of mindfulness meditation will undoubtedly have a positive impact on your golf game, though its impact will extend beyond your golf game, coloring your quality of interaction with other people, work, and even technical projects. Mindfulness is how quality emerges. In everyday life we cannot rely on a pre-shot routine for the unscripted problems which confront us, whether they be figuring out a frustrating new piece of software, assembling some furniture from IKEA, or finding our way back onto the freeway after Waze leads us off the wrong exit ramp. Success in staying on track and avoiding meltdowns is much more likely when any problem is approached mindfully. Bringing a mindful presence to interactions with your family or fellow workers will help you give people your full attention instead of the occasional glance or distracted half-listening—improving your relationships. It's a wonderful capacity that resides within, and your practice of mindfulness meditation will pay off on the golf course and in your life.

═ 15 ═

Managing Yourself Between Shots

"If your mind is sleepy, wake it up. If it is distracted, calm it down. If neither, do not disturb it."
Ramana Maharshi

IN A FOUR-HOUR ROUND of golf, the actual amount of time spent in your pre-shot routine and executing your swing is small compared to the duration of the entire round. The United States Golf Association (USGA) pace of play policy for amateur golf states that a player has 40 seconds to make a stroke. So, if you shoot 90 and use your full 40 seconds per shot, you will spend one-hour shot-making out of a 4-hour round. Obviously, most of our time on the golf course is spent between shots. Golf may be social, but the game is private. Every golfer has a lot of time to spend inside their own private world of thought, and every golfer is challenged to learn how to manage this time between shots. The cumulative effect of this "private-time" thinking has a significant impact on whether we can recover our attention for the next pre-shot routine.

How many times have you said or heard other golfers declare, "I lost my concentration" after a poor shot? Well, where did it go? We mistakenly think that we lost it just prior to hitting the shot when it was probably lost before you even got to the ball. It's lost between shots, during those three hours of the round that you are not hitting shots.

What happens during that expanse of time between shots when the mind is free to roam? We may engage in superficial conversation, daydream, or skip distractedly through countless thoughts, sensations, and perceptions. We can ruminate about life's problems or obsess about some missed shots that have already taken place. Other distractions include dissecting our golf swing, anticipating our final score, or thinking about how a bad shot cost us the last hole, how much we want to beat our opponent, what the trophy will look like, or why we never even win a trophy.

Our unending stream of thoughts and associated emotions are hard to stop on command. Our concentration is usually so diffused before we even address the ball that we have trouble getting ourselves into the performance zone of our pre-shot routine. Next thing you know, the round is over, and we're sobered to look back at how many times we lost our concentration or gave up trying to recover it.

The opposite of having scattered attention is to mindfully abide in the present between shots. Abiding in a mindful state is what mindfulness meditation is all about (see Chapter 14). Once the ability starts to develop through sitting practice at home, it can be carried onto the course and further cultivated during a round of golf through what we may call "walking meditation" which does not have to look like anything out of the ordinary. What better place to practice meditation than on the golf course? There are so many people who say, "I wish I could meditate but I just don't have the time." How about a few hours every time you play golf?

We all travel between shots with our minds scattered, living in the past (you should have seen how great I played this hole yesterday) or the future (one more par and I'll close out this match). Sometimes it's not your inner voice that's distracting, but outer challenges like the gamesmanship of people you're playing with, or any number of problems that are part of daily life.

"Walking mindful meditation" on the golf course is nothing arcane or complicated. The focus can start (as usual) with breathing, but there are unlimited options including listening to a bird singing, noting the shapes of the grass or trees, feeling the pressure of your feet on the ground, or the breeze against your skin. It can be contemplating a pleasant, abstracted state of mind or a song or piece of music.

Whatever focus for meditation you choose, expect to find it hard to maintain. The standard advice is perfectly sound—simply guide your attention back to focus when you get off track. The meditative state is far preferable to having to listen to our inner "back-seat driver" telling us, "Watch out for this downhill lie" or "Last time you were at this spot you topped it." Soon enough you will encounter your golf ball and when you do, it will be much easier to transition your attention into the focused state required for your pre-shot routine. This way, once the stroke is over, you're back with yourself between shots again. Some golfers find that too much "chit-chat" during the round makes it impossible to practice focusing attention.

Practicing mindful awareness between shots can become a beautiful part of the practice of golf. Great golfers are already doing this in some form even if they don't think about it in these terms. These players have found a way to remain in a state of mind that facilitates their transition into focused performance. It's what the walk in the kingdom is all about. A good marker of your golf progress then becomes your ability to transition back and forth between awareness and action.

When you learn to focus and be better prepared for each shot, you will also begin to notice that you find yourself somehow more prepared to address problems in your life. When you walk down the fairways of life being actively mindful, you will become more aware of the beauty around you, and in your daily life, you will notice an unexpected sense of authentic connection with loved ones and friends. We can choose to be more mindfully present between the shots in our everyday lives. Golf provides hours of opportunity to develop this skill for better golfing and better living.

16

Putting:
Two Technical Foundations

Just what the golfing world needs—another essay on putting added to the endless websites, YouTube videos, books, articles, and workshops. Your mind is likely already filled with cascades of suggested putting mantras: I will clear my mind when I putt, I will think about food, I will look at the dimple on the ball, I will watch the cup, I will learn to read greens, I will have my stroke analyzed, I will believe I am a great putter, I will have a better routine, I will just step up, look, and stroke the putt, I'll change how I hold the putter, I'll change the thickness of my grip, I'll change my putter length/shape/weight, I'll buy a more expensive putter, I'll get the putter that [fill in the blank] uses, I'll go back to my old reliable,

I'll correct my unrealistic expectations, I'll do drills, I'll make 100 putts in a row, I'll draw a line on my ball, I'll change the color of my ball, I'll leave the pin it, I'll take the pin out, I won't focus so much on making the putt, I'll use will power to force the ball into the hole, and so on. How do we ever find our way through all this? And, with input on every one of these issues, and others, what's left to talk about? Somehow there always is.

To begin with, let's consider a few facts about putting. No matter how good of a putter you are, putting performance comes and goes. One notable recent example is Jordan Spieth, who went from a top 10 ranked putter (some thought the best on tour in 2020) to almost the bottom of the pack the following year. Putting can abandon you at times and is just as likely to return. While you're waiting, there is no shortage of putting drills to work on and putting advice to try out. It's also important to come to terms with the fact that no matter what you do, you will never putt like one of the prodigies. A prodigy is someone who has a special gift that science cannot fully explain. Some people just have better eye-hand-brain connections. Think Bobby Jones, Billy Casper, Jack Nicklaus, Bobby Locke, Seve Ballesteros, Tiger Woods, Tom Watson, Ben Crenshaw, and Brad Faxon. Even so, within limits, we all can certainly improve.

Are you aware of the Sunday afternoon anomaly that distorts our expectations? On Sunday afternoons the

PGA broadcast showcases the best players in the world during one of their best playing streaks, with the hottest putters going, where they seem to make everything from 4 feet to 15 feet and often beyond. This gives us a very distorted sense of the possible and what we should be able to do. The statistical data should bring us back to reality. The average percentages of making a putt comparing touring pros/scratch golfers/bogey golfers is as follows: from 4 feet: 91/85/65; from 8 feet: 52/48/27; from 10 feet: 41/37/20; from 20 feet: 15/13/6. Strive to improve but do not benchmark yourself against unrealistic statistics.

There are two technical skills, alignment and tempo, that are fundamental to any approach to understanding and improving putting.

Alignment: Alignment is the #1 priority. If your putter face is not lined up accurately, you're more likely to miss the putt. An old-fashioned but effective approach to checking alignment is to have somebody stand behind you and watch your alignment and your outcomes as you putt. Some people manage to make putts despite poor alignment, usually by last-minute adjustments of their hands, but there is too much going on to make those adjustments work consistently. Whether you are lined up to the left or right of the hole will be obvious, even if you are absolutely convinced that you are lined up straight. This illusion is very common, but you may not be aware of it because your brain may compensate for your misalignment, and you can still manage to start the ball on line and make some putts. Overall, you definitely make more putts if your putter face is aligned properly to begin with.

It is remarkable just how many people are not lined up to where they think they are, and fixing alignment can be tricky. Strangely, it's not unusual to find that even after the putter face is placed exactly on line, it will not look correct. Factors that can impact alignment include the shape of the putter head, your eyes and head position, the angle or offset of the shaft, or how you stand. If this were easy, we all would have mastered it by now. Everyone should invest time in an alignment check-up. A lot of progress can be made in even one session.

Tempo: Being the second putting fundamental, the key to putting tempo involves understanding and utilizing the physics of the pendulum. Over 400 years ago, Galileo discovered something crucial to putting. He discovered the laws that describe the motion of a pendulum. The time it takes a pendulum to swing back and forth is independent of the length of its arc. Every putter has a fixed length and fixed weight, so if you allow it to swing on its own with minimal interference, it will take the same amount of time to complete its arc whether you pull the putter back to 4, 8, 12, or 24 inches—it does not matter. Try it by holding your putter fixed between your thumb and forefinger and just letting it swing like a pendulum. The constant motion of a pendulum allows us to use the distance of the backswing as a reliable regulator of force—far more predictable than trying to create variable forces from the same length backswing. A pendulum swing also creates the proper release of the putter head.

How do you find the right tempo? The stroke of every putt, no matter the length, should take exactly the same amount of time (reflecting the physical laws of the pendulum). Each of us has an inherent optimal tempo for the pendulum motion of our putter. You should experiment to find yours. Start by downloading a metronome app on your phone. Try beginning with an initial tempo of 74 beats/minute. Help your putter to just swing at this tempo regardless of how far you take it back. You may find that 74 is a little too slow or a little too fast. Find your own best personal tempo and then use that for every putt, from one-footers to 90- footers. You will quickly learn how far back to take the putter to maintain a smoother pendulum motion using the exact tempo you set on the metronome. You will be amazed at how much easier putting becomes.

Once you know your optimal tempo frequency, you will find that it's not so easy to duplicate. So, during practice rounds, play your phone metronome app loud enough so you can hear it when your phone is in your pocket. Of course, you won't be doing this in matches, but if you start to do it frequently enough you will learn to replicate it. Engaging in consistent practice with your optimal tempo frequency will transform you into a smooth, regulated putter, with a great tempo.

It will also become easier to dial in your distance control using different length backswings. You will be creating pendulum swings rather than hits or jabs. When practicing tempo, there is no need to use a target or try to sink putts. In fact, a target just gets in the way at this point. Have fun but pay close attention and concentrate on learning the association of backswing distance to ball travel distance. While we may never become putting machines, we can greatly improve our distance calibration. Life will always present us with variables of elevation changes, varying grass conditions, grain, wind, and other factors that will keep putting as an exciting art, made easier with alignment and tempo as its foundations.

=== 17 ===

Still Looking for the Right Putter?

THE "RIGHT" PUTTER must be out there somewhere—can you, will you, ever find it? If we're honest, we're all a little envious of those who believe that they have found it and have somehow managed to keep a long-standing relationship with it. We've also all heard stories of someone winning after picking a putter off the pro shop shelf the morning of an event. At times I think that I could use a different putter at every hole and putt just as well as I usually do.

Regardless, golfers seem to form a personal relationship with their putter, far more than with the other clubs. I've heard golfers threatening to lock their putter up in the trunk of their car as a temporary punishment for too many three putts. Many people have shared with me their belief that if a putter feels as if it's being taken for granted, it might start to act up.

Finding the "right" putter would make the game a lot easier. If you believe that the right putter is out there waiting to be found, you're about to embark on an endless road—one that I've been down more than a few times. I even made a pilgrimage to Sik golf in Orlando, FL to get fit for a new putter. Sik Golf most notably fitted Bryson DeChambeau with his armlock putter. Bryson has been the technical equipment guru of professional golfers, so he must know something, right?

There's a lot going on when we putt—hands, head, eyes, arms, shoulders, torso, feet ... all of them, some of them, and so on. Chest anchored putters were banned because it was felt they provided a mechanical advantage. So, I surmised that anchoring would likely be something of value. The arm lock putter provides a type of anchoring that is legal, for now. Arm locking does take some variables out of the equation. My putter fitting was a state-of-the-art experience, very thorough, with lots of time for discussion. Of course, I brought my own putter for some head-to-head comparisons. Putting outcomes supplemented by Quintic analytics (among the most sophisticated putter analytic tools available) all clearly favored the new armlock putter. Of course, in the Sik studio, every one of my stats improved and I could see for myself that I was rolling the ball better and more accurately. At the end of my fitting process, I was convinced I was headed for a great putting future. However, I believe that I recall hearing one of the fitters say as I left "and it doesn't hurt if you believe that this works."

You probably know the ending of this story. When I finally got my custom-built armlock putter in the mail, I struggled to feel comfortable with it. In all fairness, I was warned that it would take a while to adjust. However, I could only tolerate four weeks of excessive three-putting and I put the putter on eBay and recovered my investment. I went back to my old putter which now seemed to work better than ever. The heart of a putter can be a fickle thing.

The best thing that you can do is to simply pick out a putter that you like to look at and to get it fit for the basics of length, lie angle, and alignment. Don't obsess about whether you made the right decision. Just make that decision work. Otherwise, you're headed for a garage wall lined with rejected putters.

═ 18 ═

Fore Your Health

THE WORLD HEALTH ORGANIZATION says, "There is no health without mental health." Furthermore, most of us are not aware of or taking advantage of the potential that golf has to improve mental health. In fact, it may even look like the opposite. Many golfers complain that "this game is driving me crazy." They are often frustrated on the course—swearing, grousing, rushing through the round, or are even ready to snap a club. It's quite unfortunate that a number of golfers are missing out on the opportunity to improve their mental health through golf and only allow themselves to feel gratification after "great shots."

While we can all recall incredible moments that lift our spirits, such as that effortless swing sending a ball soaring through the air, we don't have to rely on those rare moments to find mental health promotion on a golf course. All it takes is an intention to open ourselves up to the beauty of the entire experience as we walk through every round. Slow down a little, enjoy it, savor it, and be grateful for the opportunity to play.

Years from now, let alone in a few days, no one is going to remember the numbers on your scorecard. What will be remembered are the friendships you shared, the peace instilled by the nature around you, and the joy of being out there. Take some time during every round to appreciate something that is part of your present experience—the sparkling color of wildflowers, fescue waving in the breeze, a soaring bird, or the sound of a flag flapping musically on a windy day.

Pausing from time to time to be present in your surroundings allows you to escape from living inside of your head. It also stops your game from becoming an angsty grind instead of something enjoyable. As you actively draw your attention to the present, your mental health will improve and so will your golf.

═ 19 ═

Golf Is About
Doing the Right Thing

W‍E COULD all learn something from golf's "First Tee Program," which introduces young golfers to the game and its inherent values. Golf can teach us and reinforce many of life's foundational lessons. The lessons from golf are right in front of us, for everyone, of every age—and a round of golf gives us plenty of chances to see who we are.

My own initiation into golf's lessons about life came as a high schooler in Buffalo, New York. One evening I had the good fortune to walk some holes with our club professional, Alex, a native Scotsman with a thick brogue. As for me, I was just a kid trying to hit the ball farther and score lower. Daylight lingered until about 8:30 during late summer in Buffalo, and there I was, in a bunker on the 18th hole at about 8:35. With night creeping in, it was hardly possible to see the flagstick. So, after a hurried bunker shot, we agreed it was best to call it a day. As I started to walk towards the clubhouse, Alex asked me, "Laddie, where do you think you're going?" When I said, "Back to the clubhouse," he asked me "What about the bunker?" Feeling the sting of parental criticism, I answered "It's dark now, no one is behind us, so what's there to take care of? The morning grounds crew has to rake these anyway." Alex kindly said to me "Laddie, we don't rake the bunkers for other people." That lesson stayed with me forever. Only later did I figure out how much more there was to learn from golf. But one of the core lessons is: We learn from golf what the right thing to do is and we do it.

The value of the bunker epiphany stuck with me, and I began to ponder, "What are the bunkers in my life that need raking when no one is watching?" Today, we are enmeshed with many people whose integrity we depend on. During my long career as a physician, there were countless moments when I was tempted to take shortcuts, especially since much of the daily work of a doctor can start to feel like administrative add-ons. So, "raking the bunkers" for me at work was getting charts completed on time, calling people back in a timely way, reading old records for new patients, calling other colleagues to discuss a patient, or just picking up a piece of trash in the clinic hallway. However, I never forgot the value of doing things right because it's the right thing to do. Golf gave me that lesson one darkening twilight evening in an unraked sand trap.

═ 20 ═

I Just Don't Want
to Be Here Anymore

I COULD NOT have been more elated. After traveling cross-country, I arrived at one of golf's premiere venues, Torrey Pines, outside of San Diego. With a tee time on the renowned South Course scheduled for the following day, I was starting a "practice" round on the North Course. The US Open was scheduled for the coming week, so the rough was already much longer than I was used to. Feeling fortunate to be there, I teed off with high expectations. Initially, the day seemed to be on my side. The morning was a comfortable sixty-five degrees, and the marine layer was almost completely dissipated. A blue sky was starting to declare itself and there were no threats of the previous overnight showers returning. All was right with the world, even as my opening drive found the second cut of rough, only a few yards off the fairway.

However, the rough, seeming deeper now that I was in it, was soaked from the night's rain and soon became more formidable than I expected. I took out a 7 iron and hardly advanced the ball through the long, wet grass. Unwilling to just wedge back to the fairway, I tried the 7 iron again. This time the wet grass grabbed the hosel and the ball careened into the deep wet rough on the other side of the fairway. I was searching for a lost ball for what felt like an eternity. The morning quickly began to take on a different feeling than before, and I found myself asking, "What am I doing here?" I was facing a triple bogey on the opening hole that had, only moments before, seemed to offer itself so straightforwardly in front of me. I suddenly felt like I would rather be in a thousand other places, questioning my travel decision altogether.

Looking back, I now recognize my rookie club selection error on that first hole. However, my greater mistake was starting the day filled with expectations of how things *should* be instead of welcoming the challenge to remain emotionally balanced and seeing my experience as an opportunity to learn something about my game. While privately hoping for a certain score I was actually setting myself up for failure, not only in my game but in the time I was supposed to be enjoying.

Remember, "We play golf to be better people, not just better golfers." At some point in your life off the golf course, you will find yourself having a similar experience to the one I just described at the first hole. You may have gone into a work meeting expecting to make a routine presentation and all of sudden you feel hijacked by people who said they liked your idea just the day before. As you start to feel the combination of anger and resignation, you may recognize that an impending triple bogey is happening in the conference room. You just want to be somewhere else, anywhere else. That is the time to call on the skills that you've practiced on the golf course: To accept what is, regain your emotional balance, see the situation as a learning challenge, and consider whether you could have made a better club choice. Soon enough, you get the ball back in play.

We have countless opportunities to apply what we can first learn to master on the golf course in our own lives—you cannot let the score, the conditions, or where the ball happens to land determine who you are or how you feel about your morning, your day, your life.

Even the thickest wet rough should not undermine our peace of mind. The practice of acceptance, mindfulness and emotional control is a cornerstone of golf and can be brought off of the course, especially when we are unhappy or disappointed with something. Golf can be our learning laboratory for self-improvement. Becoming aware of this opportunity allows us to find a new way around the course and around many of life's challenging layouts.

$\equiv 21 \equiv$

Wherever the Ball Is
You've Got That Shot

Most golfers are not (or not yet) thinking about playing golf to become better people. Examples of the more typical questions I get as Dr Rich Golf are, "Can you just tell me how to break 80/90/100?" or "My game is worse than ever…how do I fix it for tomorrow's match?" These questions are symptoms of the old addiction to a quick tip fix.

There are many lessons to learn from golf that are far more valuable than what you'll hear from a quick technical tip. One of the most important opportunities is utilizing golf's challenges to learn to rise above our anxieties. Everyone needs to find a way to rise above the game's anxieties and life's anxieties.

I was recently coaching an accomplished business executive who was getting more serious about her golf. One day on the course, I noticed an interesting behavior pattern. Every time she hit a long approach shot, she would scoot up on the cart seat and strain to see where she ended up, on the green or in the bunker. Now, there's nothing wrong with wanting to see where the ball went. I was more concerned about her reaction. If the ball was on the green, she would show visible relief, but if she found it in a greenside bunker, she looked deflated. I stopped the cart (since no one was behind us) and asked her if she noticed what she was doing. She was aware of her eagerness to see where her shots ended up, but she was not aware of her roller-coaster of emotions, shuttling from elation to disappointment, nor was she aware of the destabilizing effect of these emotional reactions on her golf game. I said, "I know your game pretty well by now, and I can assure you that when you get up to the green... wherever your ball is ... whether it's in a bunker or in some long rough ... you've got that shot."

As she internally voiced more belief in her capabilities, she made an active effort to decrease her anticipation of and reaction to outcomes on these approach shots. She used some simple breathing techniques and mindfulness (see Chapter 14) to focus on the present. It did not take her many rounds to report that she was able to reduce her stress about where the ball ended up.

This calmer emotional space allowed her to maintain a better tempo and finish more holes while diminishing disruptive emotional ups and downs.

During a later lesson, I mentioned to her, "You know, it's great that you've made so much progress in staying within yourself and feeling confident that you "have that shot" wherever you end up. But you know this is not just about feeling like you "have the shot" on the golf course." I went on to explain the bigger picture as to why it's so important to learn how to take control of our emotions and to notice why and when we are feeling anxious. You see, golf is not the only place where these behaviors and reactions show up. Ask yourself, what are the situations in your life that you are anxiously anticipating and then reacting to with relief or dismay? Is it how people may respond to you at work? Is it some message you had to deliver to one of your children about their schoolwork? Whatever it is, the emotional rollercoaster is not good for your life and it's likely unnecessary because if you clear the emotional space, wherever you find the "ball" in your life, you have that shot.

I got a phone call from her last off-season. She told me that she had some difficult health news to share and that her doctor had discovered an enlarged lymph node that was getting biopsied. She told me that for a few days she wasn't sleeping and couldn't even think straight. Then she remembered our discussions, and the thought came to her that wherever this "ball" ended up in terms of medical news, "I've got that shot." She told me that this brought her a sense of confidence and calmness. The follow-up is that she had a low-grade focal malignancy that was successfully treated, and she said she was surprised that she had learned something so valuable on the golf course that she could carry over into her life.

— 22 —

Letter From
an Aging Golfer

INOW UNDERSTAND how much I have learned about life from golf. I now appreciate how much I have grown from golf, more than I ever did from psychotherapy or from reading. It all came down to taking advantage of the opportunities in golf to learn about myself. Sometimes I've even wondered whether the purpose of playing golf is not to actually play golf but to learn about myself.

I was not in a good place a few seasons ago. I started to feel as if my game was gone and that I could never live with the high scores that were becoming more common. I felt like perhaps it was time for me to quit. However, what kept me going was the role that golf had played in my life for so long—at this point, I was sort of addicted to it. Regardless, I just wasn't happy to be playing anymore.

I did not have that much of a problem moving to the senior division or even the super senior division. Hey, for a while, with my new equipment, I was hitting it farther than I did 20 years earlier. But as I got older, it seemed like I was facing twin problems, how to manage my aging and what to do with my deteriorating golf game. I finally had to confront the question head-on. What is golf about? I may as well have asked what life is about. We're all trying to find a way through life, a way to make sense of the good and bad breaks that we cannot explain and often feel we didn't deserve, the hazards and the penalties, the transient joys, and the frustrated expectations. Despite my growing ambivalence with the game, I still had many days when I was on the 17th hole where I did not want the round to end. Yet, we all must come to terms with coming to the end of the round, which lies somewhere ahead.

I recall you telling me that we play golf to be better people, not just better golfers. I have certainly learned more about that in the last two years. It's been a journey for me, but I've gotten to the point where I've redefined what it means to become a better golfer. I was surprised to learn that it's something I could still be engaged in but in a new way to learn more about myself. As I made those changes, I began to feel good again about being on the course. I found myself more content, and at peace. I know this has spilled over into my everyday life. I feel like I've become a better person.

Now I recognize that it's really all about coming to terms with aging. It's a good problem to have, considering the alternative. This is my time on the golf course to connect with some basic important things in life. Getting in touch with and expressing gratitude is a big part of it. There are so many simple but profound experiences to focus on. These days I take the time to appreciate just how miraculous, beautiful, and health-promoting it is to walk (when I can) or ride over the greenness of the fairways. I savor the friendship of my golf partners. I think about the challenges of my truncated golf swing as a fun way to enhance my physical mobility and flexibility. My score is no longer the issue or genuine concern.

At first, I was skeptical about this emerging new perspective. I initially thought that it was giving in or giving up. But as I gave myself a chance to be compassionate towards myself and started to embrace "the simple things" I began to enjoy golf again. Each round continued, as always, to have its own challenges. Of course, I have a storehouse of great memories that I still don't get tired of talking about. Golf changes for every player no matter what. It's not so much a matter of giving in as it is a matter of adapting by embracing a new way of playing, a new way of life.

Some of you may be thinking, "It's easy for you to play if you remain fit and healthy." What about people with emerging Parkinson's disease, tremors, neuropathy, vision deterioration, chronic back pain, or bouts of chemotherapy? Sure, a lot does depend on symptom severity and ongoing engagement with golf may not follow a straight line. A time may come for some when golf no longer feels relevant, but until then, if it ever does, all I can tell you is that remaining engaged is important. Golf can provide a way to keep going, be something to look forward to, and expand on. Golf can provide a type of movement therapy, mental therapy, or a bridge to something spiritual that is very personal. It's truly inspiring to see people with those physical challenges out on the golf course.

It is a relief to finally learn that I don't have to play a game the way other people believe it has to be played. I no longer carry the burden of trying to impress people anymore, and I wonder why I dragged that need around with me for so many years. If there ever comes a time when I can no longer pick up a club, I will know it. Then I will have to face the same challenges—this time without golf. However, that will never really be the case. I will always have the lessons the game has given me. Even now, after all these years, I have some new insight as to why this game has endured and has a glow of the spiritual surrounding it.

23

How We See Things: It's Always About Ourselves

THE 7TH HOLE at my home course is a lengthy par four. It's the #1 handicap hole. The landing area for a good drive is guarded by a large fairway bunker. From the fairway, you face a long approach shot dominated by large bunkers to the right and left of the fairway about 45 yards short of the green. Ending up in one of those leaves the hardest shot in golf—the long bunker shot, and too often, a double bogey. Those two bunkers always loomed large as I looked up the fairway.

One day I was playing that 7th hole with a great golfer and teacher. This former LPGA player watched as I was preparing to hit my second shot after a good drive. She noticed that I was about to hit a short iron to lay up. I told her that I did not want to take on the narrow strip of fairway between the fairway bunkers ahead. Here's what she told me: "As I look up towards the green from where you're standing, I see a fairway wide enough to land a 747 in." I thought, "What? What fairway is she looking at?" Then I had my "aha moment" realizing how my own fearfulness of the bunkers altered my perception of the actual width of the fairway. It was not a ribbon at all.

My lesson on the 7th hole was a powerful demonstration of the distorting impact of fearful perception of the so-called objective outside world. We generally think that our vision is a passive recording process of the world as it is. The great golf architects know otherwise, and they specialize in creating anxiety, doubts, fears, and misperceptions that can gobble up our game before we know it, unless we learn to just see things as they are. Other obvious examples that raise doubt and alter our perception are "false-fronts" on greens or bunkers that are placed well short of a green but appear to be sitting on the green's front edge. Great golf architects know how to manipulate our minds through optical illusions. One of the greatest masters of this art is Alistair McKenzie (think Cypress Point and Augusta). It's thought that his experience in the English army in the early 20th century involving camouflaging and bunkering techniques provided the basis for his deceptive genius in designing golf holes. Mr. McKenzie was able to create a canvas of bunkers of such beautiful design that we are magnetically drawn to their presence even when they are far from the line of our intended shot. Good golfers figure out the potential impact of these deceptions and learn to compensate for their distorted perceptions.

The same phenomenon happens in our everyday life. We are convinced that we are objective observers of the world laid out in front of us. We believe that we see people "as they are" and clearly hear "what they are saying." But the Architect of our world has created things in a way that are often not what they appear to be initially. What we see and what we hear are processed by our own emotional and cognitive filters all the time. Can we ever see or hear things "as they are?" Well, just like our golf experience, our own fears and misperceptions often land us in the trees or bunkers of life. The golfer who is going to eventually master the course learns not to assume that things are always as they appear. The same sentiment of perception should be considered in our everyday lives.

═ 24 ═

Do We Have to Play Cypress Point to be Happy?

O B Keeler, widely acclaimed writer for The Atlanta Journal from 1913 to 1950, and close follower and friend of Bobby Jones wrote, "Cypress Point is a dream—spectacular, perfectly designed and set about white sand dunes and a cobalt sea and studded with the Monterey cypress so bewilderingly picturesque that it seems to have been the crystallization of the dreams of an artist who has been drinking gin and sobering up on absinthe."

Cypress Point plays like a musical masterpiece. The prelude takes place through dunes, an interlude through the forest, a dunes reprise, then the climax of what is reputed to be (with apologies to Amen Corner) the finest 3 holes in golf: 15, 16, 17 set upon a wedge of Pacific cliffs. For one moment in particular, approaching the 16th tee, only the most hardened heart could resist melting into its transpersonal beauty. Finally, as a mind-altered pilgrim, you climb the cypress-lined hill of the 18th fairway to reluctantly rejoin the world as it is. The architect himself, Alister MacKenzie, noted, "I do not expect that anyone will ever have the opportunity of constructing another course like Cypress Point, as I do not suppose anywhere in the world is there such a glorious combination of rocky coast, sand dunes, pine woods, and cypress trees."

For several days after my round, the aura of Cypress Point remained vividly alive for me in a way that is hard to explain, co-existing with and brightening the world. The point I want to make today is that we do not have to play Cypress Point to find this special dimension. Access is available on any course. We just need to slow ourselves down for a moment. The $5 Nassau, the preoccupation with a particular score, and the foursome banter about sports, politics, or work will all still be there—even if you take a few seconds to appreciate that beautiful white golf ball stunningly framed by the green beneath it. We can find the portal to another dimension not just at Cypress Point but playing on a pasture (as the game originated). Any course has the ingredients needed to transform your inner world.

Only fate will determine whether you play Cypress Point. If you are provided the opportunity, you should drop everything and go. However, fate likewise determines many aspects of our family, work, and finances—and every situation in life has all the necessary ingredients we need to find our center. It's everywhere really, nothing special is needed, so we can stop looking for those miraculous experiences. They may happen or not.

═ 25 ═

Make Yourself into a Believer

WE ALL KNOW that good putters believe that they are good putters. My sister was a great golfer, but not such a good putter. She even admitted so, often saying, "I could really compete but I'm such a terrible putter." I would always respond, "…and you always will be a terrible putter if you keep believing it." It begs the question, what can we do to start believing in ourselves more positively?

I'm fortunate to play golf from time to time with a wonderful amateur golfer, Tommy, who has earned his way to the top of state-wide leaderboards many times. He is very generous with his advice if he knows you're interested, and it's offered in a way that feels sincerely supportive. When I play with him here's how it usually goes. On the first green, I hit a putt that goes 4 feet by, and Tommy says, "You put a nice roll on that putt." On the second hole, I pull my putt left and Tommy says, "I liked your tempo on that putt." On the third hole, I leave my putt 4 feet short, and Tommy says, "You lined up well on that." On the fourth hole, another miss, and another positive statement from Tommy, such as, "You made very solid contact on that putt." So, by the fifth hole, I start to believe I actually have some putting skill. I walk to the next green feeling like I am one of the best putters in the state, simply because I've heard nothing but positive statements for the prior four holes. The cumulative effect of his positive feedback is that I start to believe that I can putt and then, of course, more of my putts start going in. The message? Positive reinforcement has an impact.

I've wondered, "Why don't we create that positive feedback transformation for ourselves?" Instead, so many players miss a 3-footer on the first hole and start thinking, "Today is going to be one of those days." They then walk off the green with dread of the next 3-footer, which of course is missed, reinforcing a negative feedback loop. Instead, we need to learn to identify the positives, creating an attitude that is more likely to result in better putting. The self-transformation through positive belief is the foundation for all kinds of improvement. Thich Nhat Hanh, a wise Buddhist monk, has said, "Sometimes good things happen that make you smile, and sometimes smiles make good things happen."

= 26 =

There's Something Greater Going On

WHAT WE'RE FACING on the golf course is a lot like what we're facing in our daily lives. We tee off every morning with hopes for a great round. Unfortunately, instead of a great opening tee shot, we often start out with slow foursomes ahead of us, hitting a weak fade into the trees or a quick pull into a left fairway bunker. We play on, trying to find a way to make sense of the good and bad breaks, of the outcomes we cannot explain, of hazards and penalties that always seem to be waiting out there, and, hopefully of our share of some satisfying swings and the transient elation of sinking a few long putts.

Whatever you are facing in your game, now is the time to look at your feeling of being stuck, despite the lessons, equipment changes, and short-cut tips for game improvement. Each round offers the potential to go beyond our programmed swing patterns and to instead open ourselves to the game's higher possibilities. The first step is to consider that there is something greater than ourselves for us to discover, something we may even find on the course. If only we knew how to open our eyes to it. I think many of us know this already and have sensed it once or twice.

One perfect New England summer day, with a cloudless blue sky and faint breeze in the low 80s, I teed off for a member-guest in an event known for its intense competitiveness, usually with some serious money at stake. That day I was not off to a good start. By the fifth hole, we were down by three, and I could not seem to recover my tempo. My usual small technical adjustments seemed only to make things worse rather than better. I started trying to try to steer the ball into the fairway, so, of course, I found myself spending more time in the woods. Yet, on the sixth hole, that forest turned out to be my salvation.

While the rest of my foursome was searching for a ball far across the fairway, I saw my own ball resting cleanly on a bed of pine needles about ten yards into the trees, illuminated by a narrow beam of sunlight that somehow found its way through the heavy pine branches. As I carefully made my way deeper into the woods, I suddenly felt immersed in the coolness of a glade. It was as if a refreshing clarity came over me, and I looked around marveling at the patterns of light and the sounds of songbirds surrounding me. Everything changed from there. After punching the ball back into play, my game was resurrected without figuring out any technical fix in particular. At the very least, I stopped all the thinking that was only compounding my problems. Maybe, I was touched by the "force" or it got in touch with me. Whatever it was, it transported me beyond my golfing difficulties and preoccupations. The scorecard started to turn around and we won the match, though that's not really the point. It was more important to be thankful for the opportunity that golf gave me to get in touch with the beauty and power that resides within.

27

Don't Make Golf a Battle with Problems

ON MANY GOLF DAYS, it can often seem as if we are facing one problem after another. No sooner do we fix the big fade with our driver than we start pulling our irons to the left. We fiddle and adjust our irons and then we lose our touch on the greens. Some days our physical balance seems out of kilter and on others, it's a problem with our timing, tempo, feel, decision-making, the randomness of bad lies, bad bounces, emotional over-reactivity, and more. It's a wonder that we can ever manage to get that small white ball into a 4¼ inch hole that's hundreds of yards away. The game can start to become a big effort and one that is sometimes not very satisfying. However, it's truly the nature of things to experience life as a series of problems. Maybe we expect too much. We often forget the perspective of Ben Hogan, "A good round of golf is if you can hit about three shots that turn out exactly as you planned them... Golf is not a game of good shots, it's a game of bad shots."

The modern approach to golf is becoming more technical, mechanistic, and, perhaps, lifeless. We may believe it possible to eventually control every aspect of the game and solve the game's problems with enough athleticism, the right equipment, sufficient discipline, and constant work. But problems will persist, regardless. Instead of fighting an end-game battle, we can try to approach the game's problems with a sense of curiosity and playfulness. Then we will be in control in a wider sense. This approach allows us to get in touch with something deeper—where everything is in balance. If you play the game without getting in touch with the background of harmony, almost everything will appear to be in the form of problems, missed opportunities, and sub-optimal shots.

One of my students was an accomplished business executive who acknowledged feeling more and more stressed by the workday's endless parade of problems. Reflecting on a time when things seemed simpler, he shared, "I can hardly get anything done now because of all these problems intruding into my work." Then one day he had the epiphany, saying, "My work is problems. That's what I do." With that insight (or "re-framing") he began to see the problems as part of the natural flow of the workplace, not a result of his lack of competence. He said he seemed to become more effective at solving these problems because he was no longer resentful of their intrusion.

If you want to play golf, you need to see that you will never overcome having problems on the golf course; they are the game itself. Just engage with each problem thoughtfully and lightly, without any thoughts or beliefs about the longer-term results. Address the challenge of each shot and then let it go without any labeling of the situation as a problem. Your mind will be in control. Of course, this switch in mentality is not so easy. The best place to always begin is with practice. This practice is the direct expression of our true nature, which started before golf was ever played and will continue into the endless future.

$$= 28 =$$

Getting Off
the Bogey Train

D ID YOU EVER find yourself on the bogey train? This experience might occur during any round when you just cannot seem to make a par. You try to engage with your pre-shot routine but somehow you feel out of sync. You can't find your swing. You've run through the list of swing shot fixes on your current list. Nothing is working and the bogies are stacking up. You try steering shots to avoid hazards, which only seems to make them more numerous and prominent. You may begin feeling sorry for yourself or resent the poorly disguised gleeful reactions of your opponents. When you've run out of ideas, here's what you can do next.

First, slow yourself down (see Chapter 4) and take some deep breaths to release physical and emotional tension (see Chapter 9). If you're still not finding your swing, it may be time to try a paradoxical approach, because the golf swing is not something you can always summon on command. You need to find a way to invite it back. Instead of fighting with yourself, let yourself (for now) accept what the day is bringing, including all those bogies. Smile at your own hubris thinking that every round can go by without some bogies. Maybe laugh at yourself for being on the bogey train when you thought you had a ticket for the par train. Sometimes, the harder you try to get off the bogey train the tighter the exit doors close. Awaken yourself from any fantasies of what your final score should be. Be patient and compassionate with yourself. You are not your golf game. Finally, you may even humbly ask the golfing gods to have mercy on you today.

From now on, instead of resentfully riding on the bogey train through to the 18th green, or feeling angry or frustrated, just let yourself enjoy the ride. You will be surprised by the effect of this apparent paradoxical approach. Soon enough, you'll find that the bogey train goes off somewhere without you. Remember, it's not just about learning to get off the bogey train on the golf course. The more important question is: what is the bogey train in your life? How do you get off that one? Try the same approach.

29

What Is the Zone and How Do You Find It?

Finding "the Zone" is a goal of every golfer, as well as every athlete, performer, and artist. When we enter "the Zone" we play our best golf, while we sense that we're a part of something that we don't quite understand. Where is the Zone and how do we find it? There is no simple set of instructions for entering the Zone. You cannot access the Zone through effort or planning. It just seems to happen. Yes, it all sounds a little mysterious and a little irrational. It is. Our instincts and education have advised us to avoid the irrational. Yet whoever has spent time in the Zone is always in search of how to get back to it. So, how do we learn to invite this irrational something into our golf game and into our lives?

Efforts to find "the Zone" have little to do with everyday problem-solving or performance psychology. We apparently live in two worlds. Most of our time is spent in the everyday golf world involving technical thinking and struggles with various thoughts and feelings. Rare intervals are spent in the Zone, where everything feels integrated, natural, and inspired. So, how can we connect these two worlds? One day this summer, during a charity golf outing, the obvious answer came to me as I stood in the shade of a large sentinel oak in the middle of a short par 4 fairway: We can create the potential bridge from our everyday world to the world of the Zone by focusing on our pre-shot routine process with quality. Pretty straightforward. Were you hoping to hear something more mystical?

What does it mean to engage with quality? Quality engagement takes discipline, mindfulness, and care to avoid things such as too many elements in our routine. What we're really practicing is a form of intense inward concentration, with curiosity and patience, avoiding self-judgments such as, "I'm just not getting anywhere with this approach." Our "practice" becomes a problem when it's layered with expectations.

On the golf course, the practice of quality processing seems to translate into rather homely advice: stick with our pre-shot routine, keep our swing in balance, breathe correctly, focus on a target, and plan where every shot will land and roll out. The Zone will find us, if it is going to. By focusing on our process, we are inviting the Zone to visit. That's the most we can do.

Through immersing ourselves in "quality processing" our golf game will improve … and, strangely, our everyday life will also improve. The patterns we establish on the golf course will start to find their way into our approach to daily life.

In our everyday life, there are always going to be those moments of stress where everything seems to conspire against us. Why is there so much traffic today? Why do they keep me waiting so long? Each of life's insults becomes a valuable learning opportunity for practicing "quality processing." We learn to be present and attentive with whatever we do, no matter how menial or trivial. When we engage in the details of the moment with quality processing, somehow things just seem to work out better. As we spend more time quality processing on the golf course, we may notice more visits from the Zone. Even without such unusual experiences as the Zone provides, we will begin to notice that something healing and peaceful comes into our golf game and into our life.

═ 30 ═

We Can't Control
Our Way to Better Golf

F OR SOME GOLFERS, the joy of the game is being displaced by the constant angst of effort—grinding all the time and obsessing about practice. Those golfers cannot conceive of playing without "trying hard all the time." Eighteen holes become a trial, a series of efforts, always thought of as culminating in some "result." Some end up clenched in this constant effort because of their personality type, and others as a result of their unexamined belief that constant effort is the only pathway to better golf.

Unfortunately, this continuous effort approach of many golfers is not leading to the hoped for results and too many aspiring golfers are burning out because of a belief that more effort is always the answer. Of course, effort is one of the required hallmarks of successful deep practice (see Chapter 5), though not for playing, including playing in competition. Ask yourself, does better golf happen as a result of effort? If it did, you could play better golf whenever you wanted, limited only by making a sufficient effort. But what happens when you try to manufacture better golf? Most often, it's impossible, and better golf may actually feel even more evasive in the face of efforts to control everything about the swing. Recently, Rory McIlroy was asked about how he was hitting so many of his great shots, and he answered, "You can't guide it. You have to trust and let go and almost give up a little bit of control to hit your best shots." Yet, many golfers approach the game as if they can perform like programmed machines.

There is another way, one where you will find that your better golf depends less on a sense of effort than on a certain presence of mind which contains within it an inherent vitality and guidance. Better golf, actually effortless golf, becomes possible when you approach the game with simple awareness focused on what is taking place right in front of you. We could also call this type of awareness "abiding" in the moment. Abiding in the moment does not mean becoming inactive or letting go of commitment to the process of a pre-shot routine. When abiding in the moment, you become identified with a silent observer that is always with you, but most often outside your awareness. This is the "you" that stands behind all your activities, that is making no efforts, remaining completely open to whatever unfolds. Can you imagine that?

Sometimes we approach our daily life with the same sense that it's a constant series of efforts because we believe we must change ourselves and our circumstances into what we think they should be. We believe that it is only effort that paves the road to happiness. We cannot conceive of living without it. After all, we need to make efforts to get those good reservations, get ourselves into the gym, and our kids into the right activities. However, life so often has its own plans. The only alternative, we're convinced, would be giving up.

Ask yourself though, does your joy in life come through effort? What happens when you try to manu-facture happiness? Most often, it's impossible. Joy and happiness may become more evasive in the face of efforts to control everything. If you can resist your habitual conviction that you need to make an effort to take con-trol of everything, even for a little while, you may be surprised to find that a mysterious creative intelligence emerges. Sometimes, just try standing back and watch-ing yourself. You will notice that there is an "observing you" behind the "worldly engaged you." Allow yourself to be that observing you, and not get caught up in the lures of what surrounds you. With this practice, you may discover an interesting sense of relief and the strangest sense that things are somehow unfolding as they should, independent of us, and realize that our constant efforts to change and control things are not necessary.

═ 31 ═

Beginners Golf Mind

WE KNOW that playing golf is difficult. That's why we sign on for lessons, new gear, devices, podcasts, and so on. We keep searching as if there's some secret that we can discover if we keep trying new things. However, we can also end up overcomplicating our swing and our minds, and then our challenge becomes keeping our minds pure and unencumbered.

In Japan, there is a phrase *shoshin* which means "beginner's mind." One of the goals when playing golf is to always maintain our beginner's mind. Suppose you have a great swing and hit a pure shot right at the pin. We can all recall times when a great shot "just seemed to happen." But what happens when you try that twice, three times, twenty times, or more? You cannot produce that state which led to the purity of that special shot. Sometimes our game only seems to become more chaotic and crowded the more we play, the more we learn, and the more we strive to master everything.

When we try to over-analyze the complexities of that perfect swing, we start to limit ourselves. Then we start to become too demanding of ourselves, start focusing on control, and lose our original and more instinctive approach to the game. In the beginner's mind, there is no thought of "I am attaining something." Such self-centered thinking limits the potential contained within our vast minds. When we have no thought of achievement, no thought of the ego in control, we become true golfers. Then we can really learn something.

There is no need to have a deep technical understanding beyond a certain point. You should not think, "Now I know how to play golf" or "I am becoming a better golfer." Yet, most golfers hit a good shot and the first thing they say is, "Look what I did (with emphasis on "I"). Instead, consider that the one real secret of the art of golf is to always feel like a beginner.

═ 32 ═

Your Posture Matters

THERE ARE countless articles and videos on the subject of "correct" golf posture, not the least of which is Ben Hogan's classic chapter on stance and posture in *Five Lessons: The Modern Fundamentals of Golf*. This essay is intended to promote awareness of posture in golf and life and how posture connects us to ourselves and to the world around us. How we hold ourselves physically, our posture, is our interface with the world. Our posture expresses and reflects the connection between our inner mental world and our outer physical and natural world beyond. Thoughtful posture becomes more and more of a challenge as we accumulate bad habits from sitting, slouching, or laziness. The impact of aging on our posture presents special challenges and often requires some combination of corrective attention along with ongoing accommodation.

In golf, there are certain consensus guidelines for addressing the ball that emerged because they facilitate a free and fluid swing. Examples of consensus basics include holding your arms freely and easily, and slightly away from your body, and taking a well-grounded athletic stance that prepares you for the action to follow. Hunching over the ball is not going to work. When you address the ball, your feet are generally comfortable at shoulder width. Pay attention to activating your core.

One of the most important components of the golf swing is maintaining a more or less straight spine and maintaining that at a consistent angle during the swing. This allows us to breathe properly, maintain our physical and mental balance, and return the clubhead to the ball where it started from. However, we all need to find our own best way to address the ball, most natural for our particular body.

No golf swing is going to work without balance. Finishing in balance is one of the great challenges and one of the great satisfactions of the golf swing. We can fall out of balance anywhere during the swing. It is worth taking some time to observe your swing and to note where you remain in balance or lose balance. How is your balance at the top of the backswing or at the finish? Balance tends to decline with age or with various health conditions. Everyone's balance can be improved with some ongoing practice. Numerous golf balance exercises are available on the Internet.

When we work on balance, we are working on both our inner and outer life. Regarding our outer life, working on balance will not only promote a better golf swing but will lessen the chances of falling or injury in every other situation we confront. For our inner life, work on balance becomes a centering, mindfulness exercise which concurrently reduces chaotic thinking and emotions. There are opportunities to work on balance almost anywhere, anytime. Try standing on one leg when you brush your teeth or when you're waiting in line. Get out of your chair for a while and challenge your balance when watching TV. Practicing balance will definitely pay off in the future as well as right now.

The golf swing can also be improved by working on body flexibility. You're not likely to be able to maintain spine angle and balance without some flexibility. As with balance, aging is not our friend. Aging stiffens us, which requires daily, thoughtful, corrective action. We also engage in sedentary lifestyles which contribute to a lack of flexibility. Your golf, and your life, will improve if you get involved in regular flexibility activities, whether you call it stretching or yoga. Whatever program you undertake you will need to be patient and consistent.

This is not a sprint. It would be ideal to adopt a flexibility program as part of lifestyle change. I know…one more thing to add to a schedule that's overfilled already. We make choices. Some people decide to shorten their aerobic workout a little to add on some flexibility exercises at the end when the muscles are already warm and receptive. A commitment to improving flexibility is a lifestyle change that will pay great dividends. Being able to increase your turn and backswing distance by even a few centimeters can add yards to your drive.

Balance and flexibility capabilities have a lot to do with posture and the golf swing. As we look around the golf course, we see players shooting low scores who don't seem to pay any attention to posture, balance, or flexibility. Youth has a great advantage. However, watch who maintains their game with aging. Watch what Bernhard Langer, Gary Player, Miguel Angel Jimenez, or Vijay Singh have been able to do as they got older because of their commitment to conditioning basics.

You should not try to copy the exact swing or stance of others—you are an individual and your stance must be the expression of your nature. The purpose of having your own right posture, based on the proportions of your own body, and your own way of standing, allows each of us to express ourselves most freely and is an important step in owning your swing (see Chapter 5).

To take the correct posture is not simply a means to an end of producing a great shot. The correct stance, and all that it entails, is itself a core component of our practice. It is the summation of your commitment to maintaining strength, balance, and flexibility through self-respect. The golf stance should be the perfect expression of your nature. When you have the correct stance, it will also produce the right frame of mind, so there is no need to try to attain some special state to be ready for your most effective golf swing. Assuming the right stance and posture will keep your mind from wandering and focus your attention. All you need to do is maintain the right posture and you have your world and mind right there.

It is important to own your posture. The moment your spine begins to curl is the moment you begin to lose yourself. Your mind will be wandering somewhere else, which will never be beneficial because golf requires you to be present here and now. Once you start to pay attention to your posture and balance, a good swing is far more likely to happen. When you stand in the right way, everything else will be organized.

So, try to adopt and keep the right posture, not only when standing over a golf ball, but in all your daily activities. Adopt the right posture when you walk, wait in line, drive your car, and when sitting and reading. If you cannot be satisfied with just doing this, it means your mind is wandering. With more awareness of the right posture, an effective golf stance is likely to follow and then there is no need to talk about the right golfing state of mind; you will already have it.

⹀ 33 ⹀

Some Zen Principles
for Golf

TRADITIONAL and modern Zen teachings have become incorporated into mainstream golf psychology. Today, it's not unusual to hear Zen-inspired philosophy being utilized to counteract overly conceptual mindsets that can constrain golf performance.

Brief statements adopted or adapted from Zen teachings seem to have powerful catalytic effects on us and can even improve our golf game. Zen-inspired reflections that seem to resonate with so many golfers often contain paradoxes such as "to get more control of your golf ball, you have to give up control." Or "seeking success guarantees failure." Or "stop seeking results if you want to improve your score." Somehow, these paradoxical statements resonate and intrigue golfers who maintain an openness to engaging with anything that might help them improve. Remember, "by not making the score the main point of your game, you will shoot a lower score." How interesting it is to see how easily Zen reflections naturally line up with golf. I know that I've found these statements immensely helpful, and I've seen so many others tune into and benefit from them.

"What is the one golf thought that always works? No thought." Most golfers understand this right away and may adopt the spirit of it during a round when nothing else is working. We can learn that our cascades of distracting thoughts can ruin a golf swing and ruin a round, so any way to remind ourselves to stop overthinking can be tremendously helpful, though the mystery of "no thought" remains ever elusive. Perhaps this could be called Zen cognitive therapy rather than Zen philosophy.

"You can be a master of golf without shooting low scores." Now this one is more challenging to talk about. Most golfers find this either confusing or absurd. What else is the purpose of the game if not to shoot a lower score? The statement could make sense as a moral lesson, where we accept that the effort to improve ourselves is what golf is about. A golfer who furthers self-awareness, who learns the right ways to behave towards others, who acquires discipline and humility, graciousness, and gratitude, and becomes transformed by the beauties encountered on the course—that person may indeed become a "master of golf" in one sense. Yet there is something in this statement about golf mastery that pushes the metaphor of golf's transformative powers to the limits. There is a suggestion that golf can become a vehicle for self-transformation in the way of swordsmanship, archery, flower arranging, or martial arts.

Many golfers are on an endless quest to keep improving but they fail to go far enough. If they want to keep improving, they inevitably have to look within and confront the whole idea of what "improving" means, beyond shooting a lower score. The "trying to do something" is the accomplishment itself. The quest for improvement seems built into golf. However, trying with the belief that you will finally attain what you want is condemning yourself to a lifetime of dissatisfaction. Hitting the ball, hitting the green, and sinking the putt is not the true purpose of golf. The true purpose is to see things as they are and to learn to let everything go as it goes. Play golf without any expectations—but this does not mean playing without any purpose. The purpose is to find out how to be yourself despite the limitations of the game: To play golf is the purpose of golf. It can be confusing for golfers to hear that they should stop making any effort to play good golf. That generally proves impossible, anyways. What we should strive for is to make an effort but forget ourselves in the effort we make. It's hard to forget ourselves when we continue to insert ourselves into everything. Look at that great shot that **I** just hit. **I** am playing great/poorly today. Leave out the **I,** and your golf game will get much better.

Now we are beyond golf—but golf can be used for this pivotal issue. There is, of course, something "deeper" to Zen teachings than we hear from golf psychology. The Game of Golf itself contains a wellspring of Zen wisdom. Zen teaching points to "truth" about who we are and our "reality" that cannot be put into words or formed into concepts. Remember, "the moment we think we have arrived, we most certainly have not," and for those so inclined to explore further, another stage of the journey lies ahead. Zen golf. I can't say what it is, or what it is not.

— 34 —

Asking
the Right Questions

A GOLFER complained that he hits unexpected duck hooks at the worst possible moments, usually into hazards. The penalty strokes kept adding up. He's spent many years hoping that someone will finally provide the right golf tip that changes everything. He keeps tinkering, holding onto the belief that he can find the fix. Yet, every time he thinks he's figured it out, another problem arises in place of the one that's just been fixed. So, he keeps looking for answers. We all keep searching for new variations of answers to the question every golfer asks, "What do I need to do now to improve my game?"

We all ask questions about our golf swing but maybe they're not the right ones. A different question to consider is, "Who keeps asking these endless questions?" Or "Who keeps trying to improve?" We're looking for lower scores and longer drives, but we're looking for the wrong things if that's ALL we're looking for. That does not mean that those things cannot be our intention. But understand that we are never going to hit the ball as far as we want or make as many putts as we want.

At some point, you must consider that the answers you are looking for are inside of you. So, one of the most important questions becomes, "Who is asking all these questions?" Try turning your thought back on itself to try and find an answer to that question. Because we reject the idea that inner peace is ever possible, we inevitably turn again to the standard approach we've repeated for years, which is to reach for more satisfaction through more accomplishment. Instead of considering that we may be asking the wrong questions, we hold on to the belief that we will feel better about ourselves when we play better and when we finally get the right advice.

POSTSCRIPT

Gardner Dickinson was a student of Ben Hogan and a 7-time PGA tour winner. His last win was over none other than Jack Nicklaus in a sudden death play-off in the '71 Atlanta Classic. He notably stated, "They say golf is like life, but don't believe them. Golf is more complicated than that."

You may not figure everything out.
You may not be a master golfer.
But to practice golf even if imperfectly is a treasured gift.
J. Silverman